ACHIEVE
The Tricky Bits
Mathematics
Practice Questions

Rising Stars UK Ltd., 22 Grafton Street, London W1S 4EX

www.risingstars-uk.com

All facts are correct at time of going to press.

First published 2008
This edition 2010

Text, design and layout © 2008 Rising Stars UK Ltd.

Written by: Sam French
Series editor: Richard Cooper
Illustrations: J B Illustrations
Design: Neil Hawkins
Cover design: Burville-Riley Partnership

Rising Stars are grateful to the QCA for permission to reproduce the following Key Stage 2 past test questions:
p17 Paper A Q21 (2003); p25 Paper B Q13 (2000);
p27 Paper B Q16 (2000); p29 Paper B Q22 (2003);
p30 Paper B Q22 (2000); p32 Paper C Q14 (2000);
p40 Paper A Q21 (2003).

British Library Cataloguing in Publication Data
A CIP record for this book is available from the British Library.

ISBN 978-1-84680-656-8

Printed by Craft Print International Ltd, Singapore

Contents

The answers can be found in a pull-out section in the middle of this book.

Problem solving 1

1 Here is a 'think of a number' puzzle.
Follow the instructions in turn.
Write your answer in the box at the end of each line.

Think of a whole number between 1 and 4.

Double your number.

Add 3 to your last number.

Double your last number.

Add 2 to the last number.

Divide the very last number by 4.

Take away the number you started with.

Is your answer 2? Write in yes or no.

1

1 mark

2 On sports day, the children in Albany School get points for each event they take part in. This table shows the points they get depending on how far they jump.

Standing long jump	
over 80 cm	1 point
over 100 cm	2 points
over 120 cm	3 points
over 140 cm	4 points
over 160 cm	5 points
over 180 cm	6 points

a) Tom jumped 138 cm.
How many points did he get?

2a

1 mark

b) Harry said 'I jumped 1.5 metres. I get 4 points.'
Give a reason why Harry is correct.

2b

1 mark

4

3 127 children visit a museum. They go in groups of 15. One group has less than 15 children. Every group of children has one adult with them.

a) How many adults will need to go?
Show your method.

| |
| |

3a
1 mark

Mrs Hunter buys 7 drinks at 64p each and 8 drinks at 72p each.

b) What is the total cost of the drinks?
Show your method.

| |
| |
| |

3b
1 mark

4 Tom and Mary went to the fair. They both had £10.00 to spend.

| **Big Dipper £2.25** | **Waltzer £1.50** |

| **Ghost Train £2.50** |

| **Roundabout £1.80** | **Big Wheel £1.75** |

a) Mary went on each ride.
How much did this cost?

| |

4a
1 mark

b) Tom had two rides on the Big Dipper and two rides on the Waltzer. Did he have enough money to ride on the Ghost Train?
Show your method.

| |
| |
| |

4b
1 mark

Total marks for this topic

5

Problem solving 2

1 Five children collect money for a charity appeal.
Here is a bar chart of the amounts they have raised so far.
Their target is to collect £50.
How much more do they need to collect to reach the target?

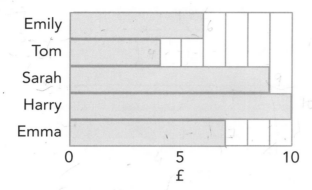

1

1 mark

2 Six people pay £4.40 each for a meal in a restaurant.
They leave a 10% tip for the waiter.
How much change do they receive from a £50 note?
Show your method.

2

3 marks

Total marks for this topic

6

Creating an aquarium

1 Lola is creating an aquarium in her bedroom.
First, she has to buy all the equipment.

The fish tank costs £39.99. Gravel is 50p per 100 g pack. Each fish is 75p and each plant is £1.

a) She buys the tank and 10 fish. How much does that cost?

1a

1 mark

b) Her tank needs 650 g of gravel. How many packs of gravel will she need?

1b

1 mark

c) The shopkeeper tells her that she should buy 5 plants for the fish tank. Add the cost of the plants and the gravel to find the total cost of the tank.

1c

1 mark

d) Lola has been saving £5 a week to buy her fish tank. How long has she been saving?

1d

1 mark

Total marks for this topic

7

Laying a garden path

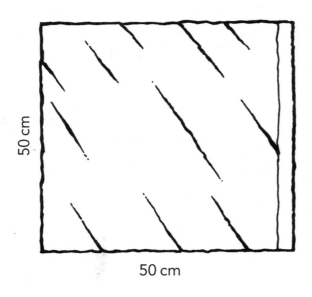

50 cm

50 cm

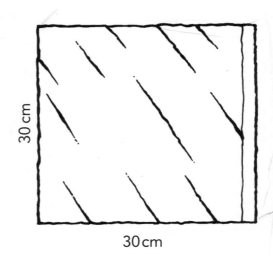

30 cm

30 cm

1 Molly wants to lay a garden path.

Her garden is 60 m long.

She has two options of paving stone. One is a square slab with a length of 50 cm. The other is a square slab with 30 cm sides.

a) How many of the larger slabs will she need to lay the path?

1a

1 mark

b) How many of the smaller slabs will she need to lay the path?

1b

1 mark

c) Larger slabs cost £1.40 and smaller slabs cost 95p. Which slab will be the cheaper option for laying Molly's path?

Show your working out.

1c

2 marks

Total marks for this topic

Going to the zoo

1 Class 6F are going on a school trip to the zoo. There are 30 children in the class and 5 adults accompany them.

Children's tickets are £4.50 and adults' tickets are £6.00. However, because it is a school trip, 1 adult for every 10 children gets in free.

a) How much will the school trip cost? Show your working out.

1a

2 marks

b) Whilst at the zoo, there are three activities to choose from; $\frac{1}{2}$ the class go to the sea lion show and $\frac{1}{3}$ go to the reptile house. How many visit the big cats?

1b

2 marks

c) What fraction of the class visit the big cats?

1c

1 mark

d) The class leave school at 8.45 a.m. and get back to school at 4.20 p.m. How long are they on their trip?

1d

1 mark

e) The coach trip takes 50 minutes each way. How long were they at the zoo?

1e

1 mark

Total marks for this topic

9

Fractions

1 Calculate:

a) $\frac{2}{5}$ of £2.50 =   £ ☐

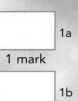
1a
1 mark

b) $\frac{3}{4}$ of £4.80 =   £ ☐

1b
1 mark

c) $\frac{3}{10}$ of 2 litres = ☐ millilitres

1c
1 mark

2 a) What is $\frac{3}{7}$ of 28?

☐

2a
1 mark

b) What is $\frac{4}{8}$ of 81?

☐

2b
1 mark

c) What is $\frac{2}{5}$ of 250?

☐

2c
1 mark

d) What fraction of 100 is 17?

☐

2d
1 mark

e) Use the symbols < or > to make the following statements correct.

i) $\frac{1}{2}$ ☐ $\frac{1}{3}$ iii) $\frac{1}{6}$ ☐ $\frac{3}{12}$

ii) $\frac{3}{10}$ ☐ $\frac{1}{4}$ iv) $\frac{9}{10}$ ☐ $\frac{4}{5}$

2e
1 mark

Total marks for this topic   ☐

Mixing paint

Leo wants to make some purple paint. He knows he can make purple by mixing red and blue paint in the ratio of 4:5.

a) He has 12 litres of red paint. How much blue paint will he need?

| |
| |

1 mark ___ 1a

b) How much purple paint will that make?

| |
| |

1 mark ___ 1b

c) Leo needs 36 litres of purple paint. How much red and blue paint will he need?

| |
| |

1 mark ___ 1c

d) Leo finds some pots of blue paint – there are 25 litres. How much red paint will he need to buy to mix up some more purple?

| |
| |

1 mark ___ 1d

Total marks for this topic ___

Making a salad

1 Harry is making a salad.

He uses 2 lettuces, 1 pepper, 2 tomatoes and 3 onions in each person's salad.

a) If he wants to make enough salad for 9 people, how many of each vegetable will he need to use?

Lettuce ☐   Tomato ☐

Pepper ☐   Onion ☐

☐ 1a

2 marks

b) If Harry had 45 onions, how many salads could he make?

☐

☐ 1b

1 mark

c) In total, Harry has 48 vegetables. He uses them all to make some salads. How many complete salads does he make?

☐

☐ 1c

1 mark

Total marks for this topic ☐

Going to the cinema

1

a) In a cinema, there are 5 children for every 2 adults. There are 12 adults in the audience. How many children are there?

1a

1 mark

b) In a different showing of the film, the child to adult ratio is the same as before. There are 105 people in the screening. How many of them are adults?

1b

1 mark

c) Two children in the cinema eat popcorn, for every 3 that have an ice-cream. If 36 children eat an ice-cream, how many would have popcorn?

1c

1 mark

d) The cinema sells 2 drinks – cola and orange – in a ratio of 3:4. If the cinema sells 56 drinks in total, how many of each drink does it sell?

1d

1 mark

Total marks for this topic

13

Missing numbers and using brackets

1 Fill in the missing numbers in the boxes.

a) (☐ × 9) ÷ 6 = 6   **b)** 6 × (9 ÷ 3) = ☐   **c)** 4^2 ÷ ☐ = 2

1

1 mark

2 Fill in the missing numbers in the boxes.

a) (3 + 2) × 5 = ☐   **b)** (☐ + 6) × 8 = 64

c) (19 × ☐) + 25 = 101

2

1 mark

3 Calculate:

a) (4 + 2) × 3 = ☐   **b)** 4 + (2 × 3) = ☐

3a

1 mark

c) Work out the answer to: (3 + 4) × (4 + 5 + 1)
Show your method.

☐

3c

1 mark

d) Put brackets in this calculation to make the answer equal to 60.

5 + 6 + 1 × 5 = 60

☐
3d

1 mark

e) Put brackets in this calculation to make the answer equal to 40.

5 + 6 + 1 × 5 = 40

☐
3e

1 mark

4 **a)** Write what the two missing numbers could be.

☐ ÷ ☐ = 8

☐
4a

1 mark

b) Write what the two missing numbers could be.

(6 + ☐) × ☐ = 100

☐
4b

1 mark

c) Write what the missing number is.

30 − 17 = 8 + ☐

☐
4c

1 mark

Total marks for this topic ☐

Perimeter and area

1 Each square represents 1 cm.
Find the area and the perimeter of these shapes.

a)

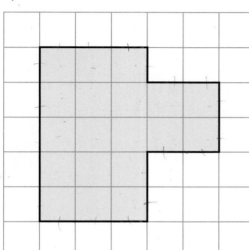

b)

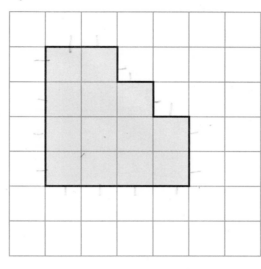

Area = ☐ cm²

Perimeter = ☐ cm

Area = ☐ cm²

Perimeter = ☐ cm

	1a
2 marks	

	1b
2 marks	

2 **a)** Here is a grid of centimetre squares.
On the grid below, draw a shape that has an area of 10 square centimetres.

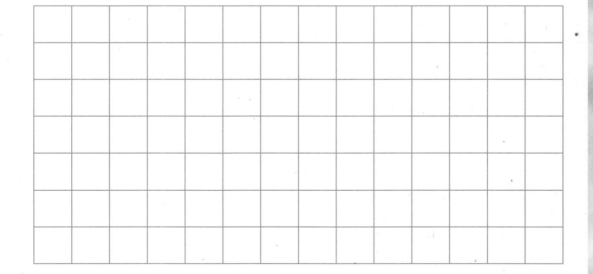

	2a
1 mark	

b) On the grid of centimetre squares below, draw a rectangle which has a perimeter of 10 centimetres.

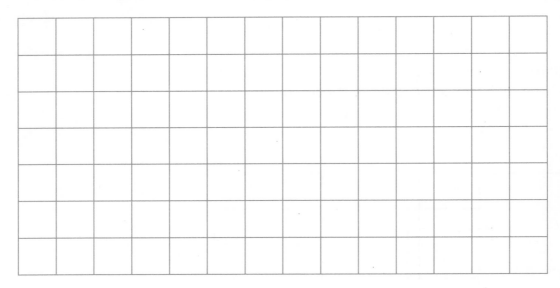

2b

1 mark

3 Here is a shaded shape on a grid made of centimetre squares.

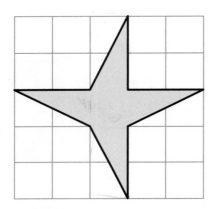

a) What area is shaded?

cm²

3a

1 mark

b) What fraction of the area of the grid is shaded?

3b

1 mark

Total marks for this topic

16

Shape and area

(1) Match each shape on the left to one with equal area on the right.

One has been done for you.

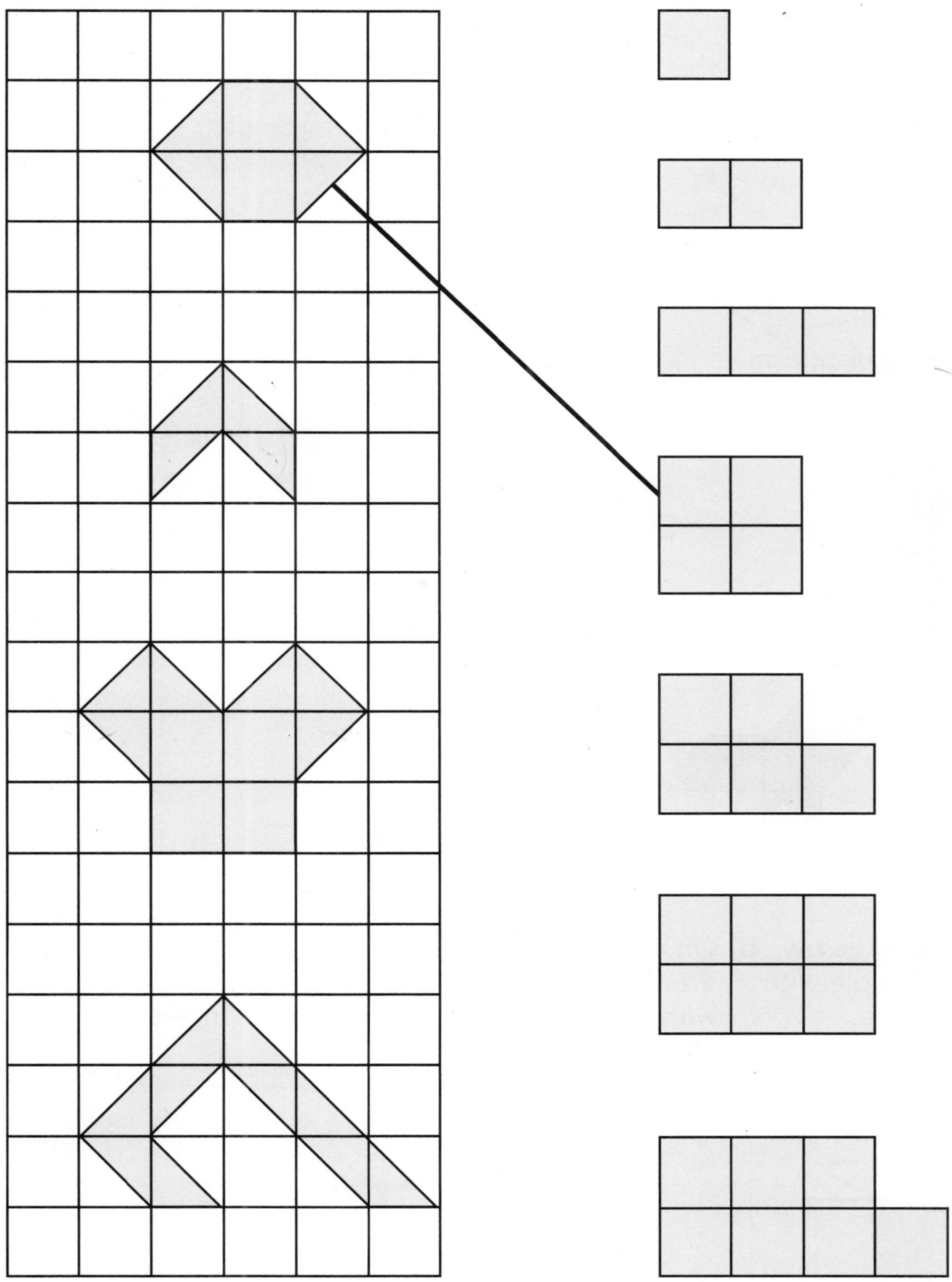

1

1 mark

Total marks for this topic

2-D and 3-D shapes

1 Here are 5 solid shapes and 5 nets. Match each shape to its net. Write the letter of the correct net under the shape.

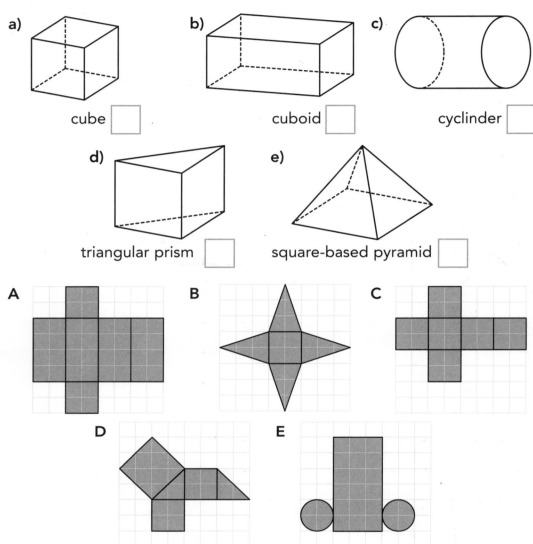

a)

cube ☐

b)

cuboid ☐

c)

cyclinder ☐

d)

triangular prism ☐

e)

square-based pyramid ☐

A   B   C

D   E

2 a) On the grid below, draw a triangle with 1 right angle.

b) On the grid below, draw a quadrilateral with only 2 right angles.

c) On the grid below, draw a pentagon with 3 right angles.

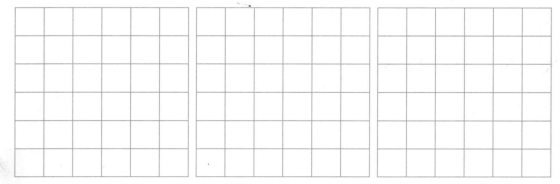

1 mark   1a
1 mark   1b
1 mark   1c
1 mark   1d
1 mark   1e

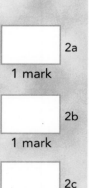

1 mark   2a
1 mark   2b
1 mark   2c

3 Look at these shapes drawn on a square grid.

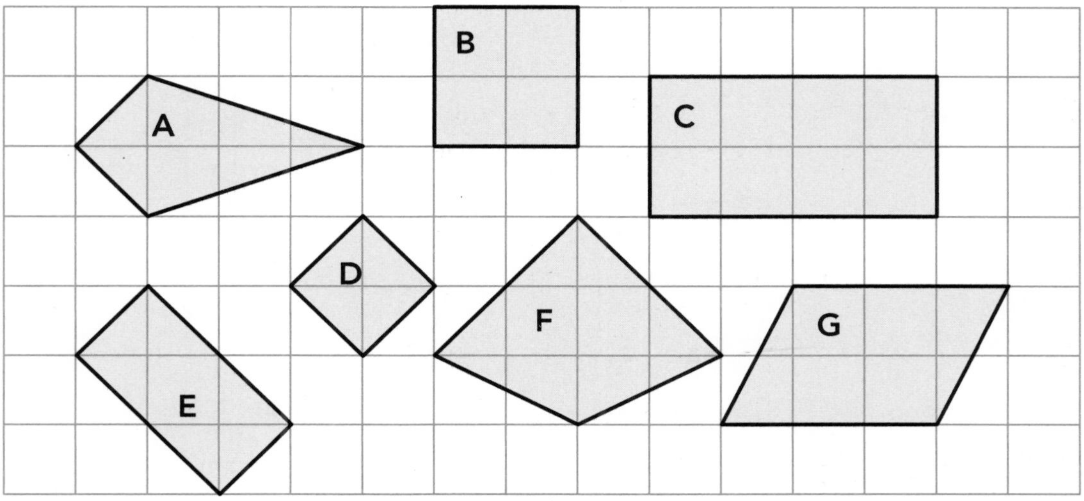

Fill in the table that sorts the shapes into groups.
Tick (✔) the box if the description fits.

Shape	All sides equal	Opposite sides parallel	All angles right angles
A			
B			
C			
D			
E			
F			
G			

3

2 marks

16

4 Harry is packing cubes into a box.

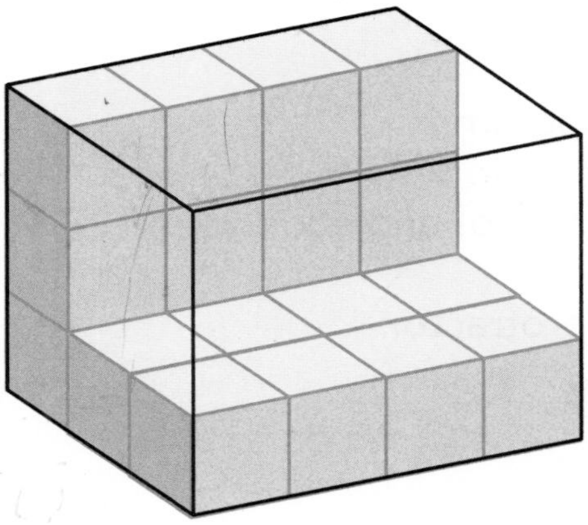

He has filled the base and one side.
How many cubes will the box hold when it is full?

4

1 mark

Total marks for this topic

Angles

(**1**) Measure this angle:

A

a) Write your answer here [　　　] °

b) On the diagram, draw a line at an angle of 50° at A to make a triangle.

(**2**) Look at the diagram:

Calculate the size of angle x
and angle y.
Do not use a protractor.

x = [　　　] °

y = [　　　] °

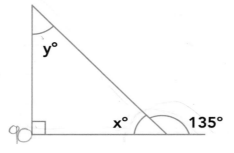

(**3**) Look at the diagram:

Calculate the size of angle x
and angle y.
Do not use a protractor.

x = [　　　] °

y = [　　　] °

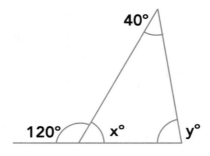

4 Look at the diagram.

Calculate the size of angle x.
Do not use a protractor.

x = [ ] °

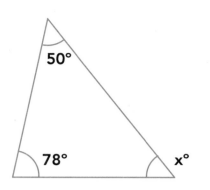

4

1 mark

5 Look at the diagram.

Calculate the size of angle x.
Do not use a protractor.

x = [ ] °

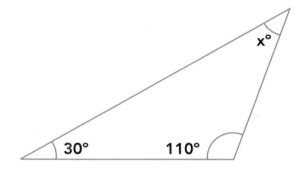

5

1 mark

6 Look at the diagram.

Calculate the size of angle x.
Do not use a protractor.

x = [ ] °

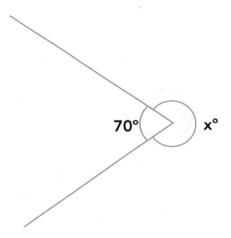

[ ]
6

1 mark

7 Look at the diagram.

Calculate the sizes of angles x and y.
Do not use a protractor.

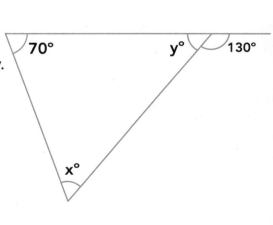

x = [ ] °

y = [ ] °

[ ]
7

2 marks

Total marks for this topic [ ]

21

Shapes, symmetry and angles

1 Look at these shapes.

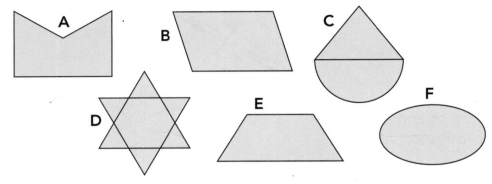

A B C D E F

a) Which shapes have one line of symmmetry?

1a

1 mark

b) Which shapes have more than one line of symmetry?

1b

1 mark

c) Which shapes have no lines of symmetry?

1c

1 mark

2 Look at the diagram.

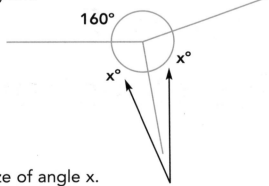

160°

x°   x°

Calculate the size of angle x.
Do not use a protractor.
Show your method.

These 2 angles are equal.

2

2 marks

Total marks for this topic

22

THE
TRICKY
BITS

MATHEMATICS
Answers for
Practice Questions

RISING★STARS

Pages 4–5 – Problem solving 1

1 *Check working*

2 a) 3 points

 b) *Example:* because 1.5 metres = 150 cm which is between 140 cm and 160 cm

3 a) *Example:* 127 ÷ 15 = 8 r5, therefore 9 adults

 b) 7 × 64 = £4.48 8 × 72 = £5.76
 £4.48 + £5.76 = £10.24

4 a) £9.80

 b) Yes
 £2.25 + £2.35 + £1.50 + £1.50 = £7.50
 £10.00 – £7.50 = £2.50

Page 6 – Problem solving 2

1 £14

2 6 × £4.40 = £26.40
 £26.40 ÷ 10 = £2.64
 £26.40 + £2.64 = £29.04
 £50 – £29.04 = £20.96

Page 7 – Creating an aquarium

1 a) £47.49

 b) 7 packs (she will have 50 g left over from the seventh pack)

 c) 47.49 + (7 × 0.5) + (5 × 1) = £55.99

 d) 12 weeks (55.99 ÷ 5 = 11.1 which needs to be rounded up to 12)

Page 8 – Laying a garden path

1 a) 12 slabs (600 ÷ 50)

 b) 20 slabs (600 ÷ 30)

 c) £1.40 × 12 = £16.80
 £0.95 × 20 = £19.00
 Larger slabs are cheaper.

Page 9 – Going to the zoo

1 a) £4.50 × 30 = £135 for the children. 3 adults free, so have to pay for 2, which is £12; £135 + £12 = £147

 b) 15 go to sea lions, 10 go to reptile house, which leaves 5 to visit the big cats.

 c) $\frac{1}{2}$ of 30 = 15

 $\frac{1}{3}$ of 30 = 10

 30 – 15 – 10 = 5;

 $\frac{5}{30}$ or $\frac{1}{6}$

d) 7 hours and 35 minutes

e) 5 hours 55 minutes

Page 10 – Fractions

1 a) £1.00

 b) £3.60

 c) 600 ml

2 a) 12

 b) $40\frac{1}{2}$

 c) 100

 d) $\frac{17}{100}$

 e) i) >

 ii) >

 iii) <

 iv) >

Page 11 – Mixing paint

1 a) 15 litres (5 × 3)

 b) 27 litres (12 + 15)

 c) 16 red (4 × 4); 20 blue (4 × 5)

 d) 20 litres (25 ÷ 5 = 5, 5 × 4 = 20)

Page 12 – Making a salad

1 a) 18 lettuces; 9 peppers; 18 tomatoes; 27 onions

 b) 15 salads (45 ÷ 3 = 15)

 c) 6 salads (48 ÷ 8 = 6)

Page 13 – Going to the cinema

1 a) 30 children (6 × 5)

 b) 30 adults (105 ÷ 7 × 2)

 c) 24 (36 ÷ 3 × 2)

 d) 24 cola and 32 orange

Page 14 – Missing numbers and using brackets

1 a) (4 × 9) ÷ 6 = 6

 b) 6 × (9 ÷ 3) = 18

 c) 4^2 ÷ 8 = 2

2 a) (3 + 2) × 5 = 25

 b) (2 + 6) × 8 = 64

 c) (19 × 4) + 25 = 101

3 a) (4 + 2) × 3 = 18

 b) 4 + (2 × 3) = 10

 c) 70

 d) (5 + 6 + 1) × 5 = 60

 e) 5 + ((6 + 1) × 5) = 40

4 a) *Example:* 16 ÷ 2 = 8

 b) *Example:* (6 + 4) × 10 = 100

 c) 30 – 17 = 8 + 5

Pages 15–16 – Perimeter and area

1 a)

Area = 19 cm²
Perimeter = 20 cm

 b)

Area = 13 cm²
Perimeter = 16 cm

2 a) *Check drawing*

 b) *Check drawing*

3 a) 5 cm²

 b) $\frac{5}{25}$ or $\frac{1}{5}$

Page 17 – Shape and area

1
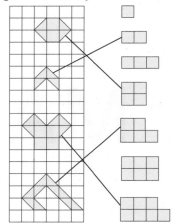

Pages 18–19 – 2-D and 3-D shapes

1 a) C

 b) A

 c) E

 d) D

 e) B

2
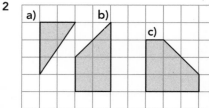

3

Shape	All sides equal	Opposite sides parallel	All angles right angles
A			
B	✔	✔	✔
C		✔	✔
D	✔	✔	✔
E		✔	✔
F			
G		✔	

4 36

Pages 20–21 – Angles

1 a) 80°

  b) Line drawn at 50° at A to make a triangle.

2 x = 45°   y = 45°

3 x = 60°   y = 80°

4 x = 52°

5 x = 40°

6 x = 290°

7 x = 60°   y = 50°

Page 22 – Shapes, symmetry and angles

1 a) A, C, E

  b) F, D

  c) B

2 2x = 200°

  x = 100°

Pages 23–24 – Cubes 1

1 a) Any of the following:

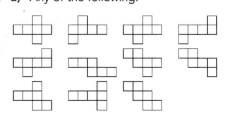

  b) One mark for each correct X.

2 a) 11

  b)

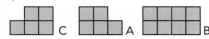

3 a) B, D

  b) D

Page 25 – Square-based

pyramids

1

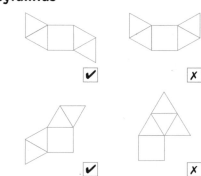

    ✔   ✗

    ✔   ✗

All correct for 1 mark.

Page 26 – Nets and shapes

1

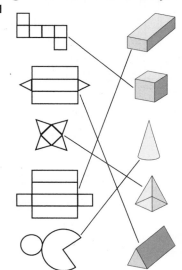

Page 27 – Cubes 2

1

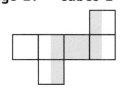

Page 28 – Reflective symmetry

1

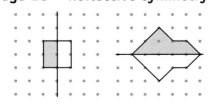

1 mark for each shape reflected correctly.

2

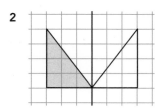

Pages 29–30 – Spinners 1

1 ✗

  ✔

  ✔

  ✗

All correct for 1 mark.

2 It is just as likely, as half of each spinner is covered by the 1.

Pages 31–33 – Spinners 2

1 a) Spinner A

  b) Because half of Spinner B is 1, and more than half of Spinner A is a 1.

  c) 1/6

  d) 1/4

  e) Yes

  f) The maximum score on each spinner is 3; so the maximum joint score is 6, which is less than 7.

2 a) Circle: YES

  b) There are 3 odds, but each is 2 points – that makes 6 for Jane. There are only 2 even numbers but Sam gets 3 points for each – that's 6 as well.

3 a) 1/2 or 3/6

  b) 0

  c) 4/6 or 2/3

  d) 1/2

  e) No. They are both equally likely – both have a probability of 1/2.

Page 34–35 – Grouping data

1 a)

Number of goals	1–5	6–10	11–15	16–20	21–25	26–30	31–35	36–40
Number of teams	0	1	3	3	7	3	2	1

  b)

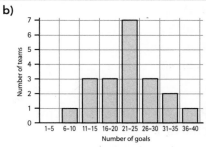

2 a) 5

  b) 6 + 8 + 7 + 5 + 2 = 28

3

Number of people	Frequency	Total
0–9	/	1
10–19	++++	5
20–29	++++ //	7
30–39	++++ ////	9
40–49	++++	5
50–59	//	2
60–69	/	1

4 a) 13

  b) apple

  c) 4 + 8 + 14 + 13 + 6 + 7 = 52

Pages 36–37 – Understanding diagrams and tables

1 a) 6

  b) 4

  c) 46

2 a) 08:03

  b) 09:30

  c) 1 hour and 27 minutes

3 a) 415 miles (1163 − 748 = 415)

  b) Venice

  c) £116 (29 × 4 = 116)

  d) £23.20 (29 × 0.8 = 23.20)

  e) number of miles × 1.6

  f)

	Barcelona	Venice	Prague
Gatwick		1470.4	1196.8
Edinburgh	2169.6	2134.4	1860.8
Paris	1118.4	1139.2	

Pages 38–39 – Graphs and pie charts 1

1 a) 19 °C

  b) 11 °C

2 Yes

  Example: same number for each in Y6, more in Y5

3 a) 6

  b) 33

4 a) walk

  b) 40

Page 40 – Graphs and pie charts 2

1 Answers between 30 and 36

2 a) %

  b) Circle: NO

  c) Half of 30 is not the same as half of 24.

Page 41 – Charts and tables

1 a) Ann – 40

    Paul – 25

    David – 20

    Jane – 15

  b)

2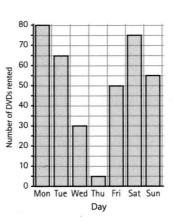

Pages 42–43 – Line graphs

1 a) 9

  b) 39.2°C Accept 39.1°C to 39.3°C

2 a) *Example*: wet and cold

  b) Friday was hotter and drier than Wednesday.

3 a) 09:00

  b) 12:00

  c) *Example*: 09:30 and 14:30

  d) 130 cm

Cubes 1

1 This is a net of a cube. There are lots of different ways of creating a net that will form a cube with a lid.

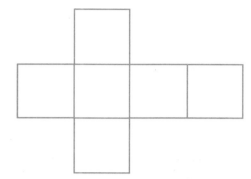

a) Use each of the spaces below to create 3 different nets that will form a cube.

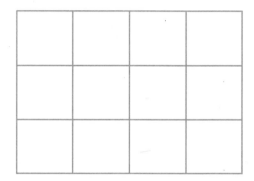 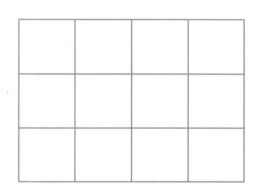

1a

3 marks

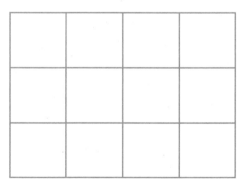

b) Put an X in the square that would form the base of each of the cubes created by each of the nets.

1b

3 marks

2 Sally is making a shape from plastic cubes.
This is the shape she makes.

A

C

B

a) How many cubes has she used?

| |
| |

2a

1 mark

b) Sally turns the shape around and looks at it in three different ways.

Here are the three pictures Sally will see when she looks at her shape; one when she looks at it from A, one from B and one from C. Write underneath each picture whether it is what Sally will see from A or from B or from C.

2b

3 marks

3 Here are some shapes made out of centimetre squares.

A   B   D

C

a) Which shapes will not fold up to make an open box?

| |
| |

3a

1 mark

b) Which shape does not have a perimeter of 12 cm?

| |
| |

3b

1 mark

Total marks for this topic

Square-based pyramids

1 Look at each of these diagrams.

Put a tick (✔) if it is the net of a square-based pyramid.
Put a cross (✗) if it is not.

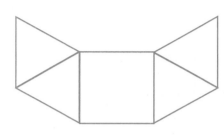

1

1 mark

☐

☐

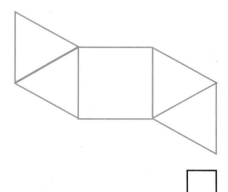

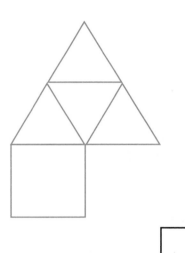

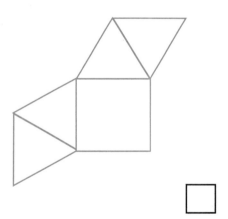

☐

☐

Total marks for this topic ☐

Nets and shapes

1 Can you match the correct net with its 3-D shape?

Draw a line from each net to the 3-D shape it makes.

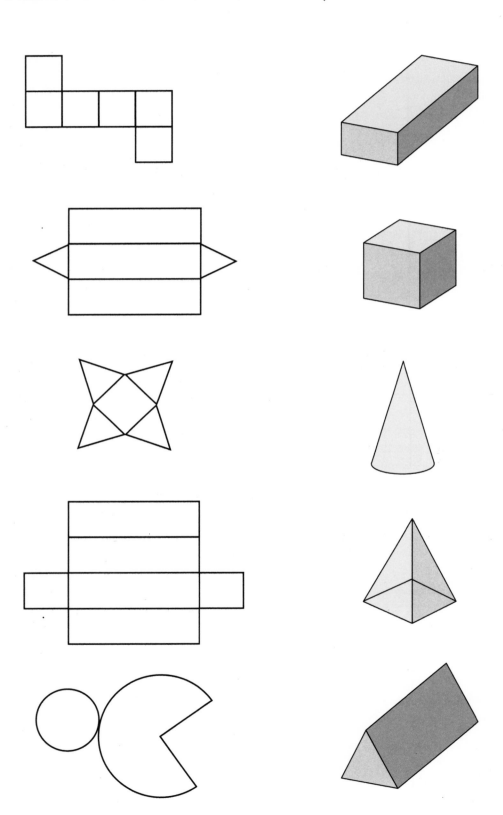

5 marks

Total marks for this topic

26

Cubes 2

1 Here is a cube.

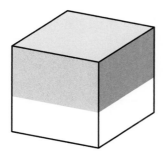

The cube is shaded all the way round so that the top half is blue and the bottom half is white.

Here is the net of the cube.

Complete the shading.

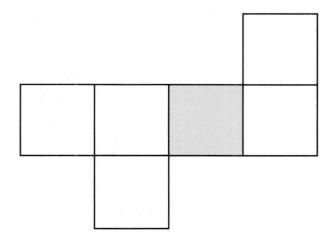

1

1 mark

Total marks for this topic

Reflection

1 Reflect each shape below in the mirror line.

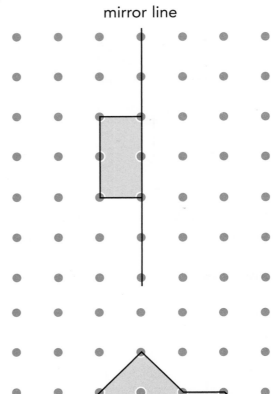

mirror line

mirror line

2 Draw the reflection of this triangle in the mirror line.

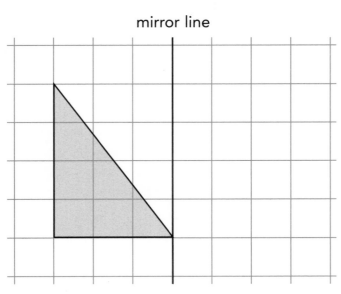

mirror line

Total marks for this topic

Spinners 1

1 Here is a square spinner.

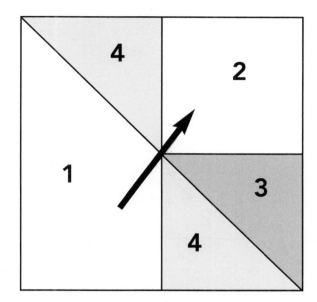

Look at these statements.

For each one put a tick (✔) if it is correct.
Put a cross (✗) if it is not correct.

4 is the most likely score.

2 and 4 are equally likely scores.

Odd and even scores are equally likely.

A score of 3 or more is as likely as a score of less than 3.

1 mark

2 Katie made two spinners, A and B.

Spinner A

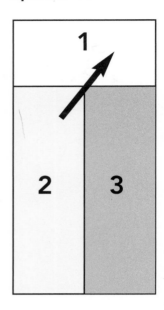

Spinner B

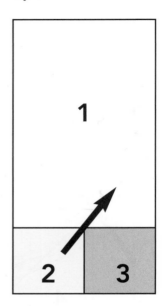

She says: 'Scoring a 1 on Spinner A is just as likely as scoring a 1 on Spinner B.'

Explain why Katie is correct.

2

1 mark

Total marks for this topic

Spinners 2

(1)

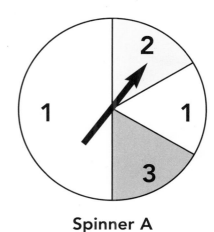

Spinner A

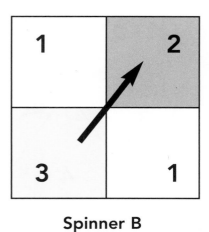

Spinner B

a) With which spinner are you more likely to score a 1?

1a

1 mark

b) Why?

1b

1 mark

c) What is the probability of scoring a 2 on Spinner A?

1c

1 mark

d) What is the probability of scoring a 3 on Spinner B?

1d

1 mark

e) Abdul spins both Spinner A and B. He says that the combined score of the spinners will definitely be less than 7. Is he right?

1e

1 mark

f) Why?

1f

2 marks

31

2 Here is a spinner with five equal sections.

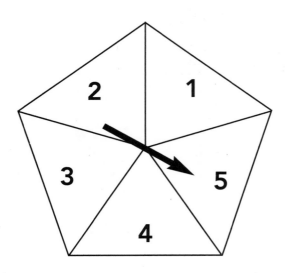

Jane and Sam play a game.

They spin the pointer many times.

If it stops on an odd number, Jane gets 2 points.

If it stops on an even number, Sam gets 3 points.

a) Is this a fair game? Circle Yes or No.   YES   NO

2a

1 mark

b) Explain your answer.

2b

1 mark

(3)

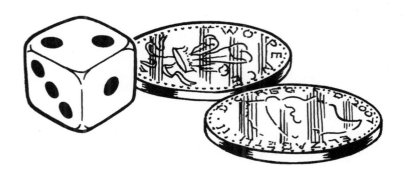

Faika rolls a dice.

a) What is the probability of her rolling an even number?

| | 3a |
| 1 mark |

b) What is the probability of her rolling a 7?

| | 3b |
| 1 mark |

c) What is the probability of her rolling a number less than 5?

| | 3c |
| 1 mark |

d) At the same time, Grace tosses a coin.
What is the probability of her coin landing heads up?

| | 3d |
| 1 mark |

e) Faika says she is more likely to roll an odd number than Grace is likely to toss a tail.

Is she right? Explain why.

| | 3e |
| 2 marks |

Total marks for this topic

33

Grouping data

1 Here is a list of the number of goals scored by the end of January by the teams in a football league.

32   28   14   8   15   22   22   24   39   20

20   24   26   25   23   21   14   35   26   19

Kevin puts the numbers in groups in a table.

a) Fill in the missing numbers in the table.

Number of goals	1–5	6–10	11–15	16–20	21–25	26–30	30–35	36–40
Number of teams	0	1	3	2	7	3	2	1

1a
1 mark

b) Use the table to complete the bar chart.

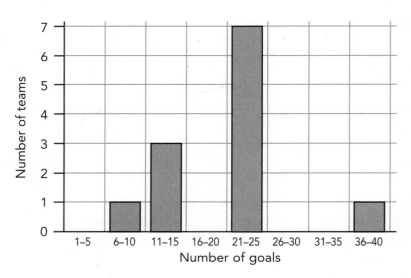

1b
1 mark

2 This bar chart shows the number of pets owned by the children in Class 7.

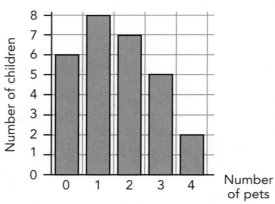

a) How many children have 3 pets?

2a
1 mark

b) All the children in Class 7 took part. How many children was this?

2b
2 marks

34

3 Some children counted the number of people going into a library every day between 9 a.m. and 2 p.m. for one week.

	9 a.m. – 10 a.m.	10 a.m. – 11 a.m.	11 a.m. – 12 noon	12 noon – 1 p.m.	1 p.m. – 2 p.m.
Monday	15	26	12	32	8
Tuesday	16	39	63	21	36
Wednesday	29	36	56	18	43
Thursday	31	40	44	31	26
Friday	45	49	58	38	20
Saturday	38	25	37	29	19

Complete the frequency table. Some of the entries have been done for you.

Number of people	Frequency	Total
0–9		
10–19	|)	
20–29	∦ // |	7
30–39		
40–49	∦	5
50–59		
60–69		

4 Amy asked some people about their favourite fruits. This bar chart shows how they answered.

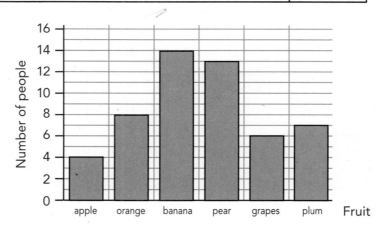

a) How many people chose pears?

b) Which fruit was chosen by the fewest people?

c) How many people did Amy ask?

Total marks for this topic

Understanding diagrams and tables

1 This diagram shows the number of flower beds in the local park. Some flower beds have only one colour of flower in them; some have more than one colour.

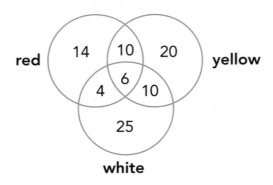

a) How many flower beds have 3 colours of flower in them?

	1a

1 mark

b) How many flower beds have only red and white flowers in them?

	1b

1 mark

c) How many flower beds have yellow flowers in them?

	1c

1 mark

2 This timetable shows the times of trains from Derby to London.

Derby	06:33	06:56	07:56	09:01
London	08:33	08:53	09:33	10:41

a) The train due to leave Derby at 07:56 actually left 7 minutes late. What time did it leave?

	2a

1 mark

b) The same train arrived in London 3 minutes early. What time was that?

	2b

1 mark

c) How long did the journey take?

	2c

1 mark

3 Air miles between each city (distances in miles) are shown in the table.

	Barcelona	Venice	Prague
Gatwick	940	919	748
Edinburgh	1356	1334	1163
Paris	699	712	496

a) Gatwick is nearer to Prague than Edinburgh is. How many miles nearer is Gatwick?

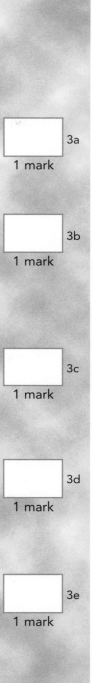

3a

1 mark

b) Which city is furthest away from Paris?

3b

1 mark

c) Star Airlines offers seats from Gatwick to Barcelona for £29 per person. How much will it cost for 4 adults to fly from Gatwick to Barcelona?

3c

1 mark

d) Star Airlines offers a 20% discount for children. How much is a child's fare to Barcelona?

3d

1 mark

e) 1 mile = 1.6 km
How will you convert miles into kilometres (km)?

3e

1 mark

f) Rewrite the distance in the table in kilometres. (You can use a calculator.)
Two have been done for you.

	Barcelona	Venice	Prague
Gatwick	1504		
Edinburgh			
Paris			793.6

3f

3 marks

Total marks for this topic

37

Graphs and pie charts 1

1 This graph shows the temperature in London for one day in June.

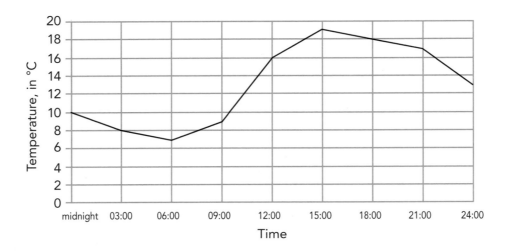

From the graph:

a) What was the temperature at 3 p.m.?

[ ] °C

b) How much hotter was it at 18:00 than at 06:00?

[ ] °C

2 A school has the same number of pupils in Years 5 and 6.
The headteacher asked these pupils:

"Should we go to the theme park or
the seaside for a trip?"

The diagrams show the results from
each year group.

Amy said: "Altogether, the theme
park was more popular."

Was she correct? Tick (✔) Yes or No.

Yes [ ]   No [ ]

Explain your answer.

Year 5

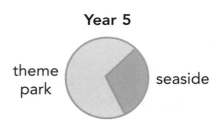

theme park — seaside

Year 6

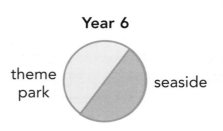

theme park — seaside

3 Sally asked the children in her class what their favourite colour was. She has drawn a bar chart of her results.

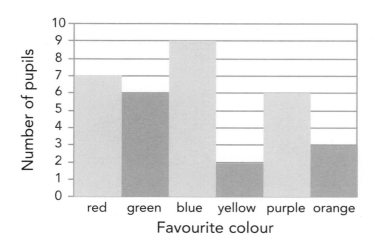

a) How many children chose green?

3a
1 mark

b) How many children were there in Sally's class?

3b
1 mark

4 The pie chart shows how all the pupils travel to a small village school.

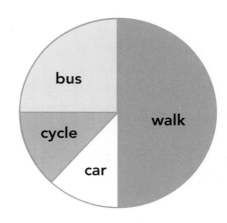

a) Which is the most popular way of coming to school?

4a
1 mark

b) If 10 children travel by bus, how many children are there in the school?

4b
1 mark

Total marks for this topic

Graphs and pie charts 2

1 The pie charts show the results of a school's netball and football matches.

Netball

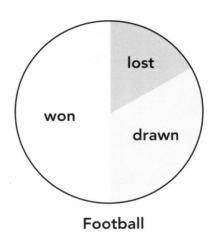

Football

The netball team played 30 games.

The football team played 24 games.

Estimate the percentage of games that the netball team lost.

%

1

1 mark

2 David says: 'The two teams won the same number of games.'

Is he correct?

a) Circle Yes or No.   YES   NO

2a

1 mark

b) Explain how you know.

2b

1 mark

Total marks for this topic

40

Charts and tables

1 This pictogram shows the number of comics some children in Class 6 had.

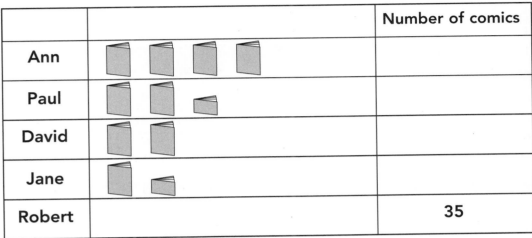

		Number of comics
Ann		
Paul		
David		
Jane		
Robert		35

 represents 10 copies   represents 5 copies

a) How many comics does each child have? Complete the pictogram.

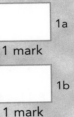

1a

1 mark

b) Complete the pictogram showing the number of comics Robert has.

1b

1 mark

2 This table shows the number of DVDs rented from 'Premier DVDs' in one week in December.

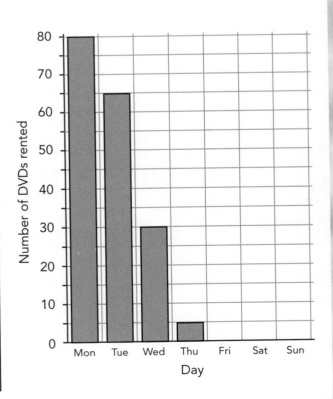

Day	Number of DVDs rented
Monday	80
Tuesday	65
Wednesday	30
Thursday	5
Friday	50
Saturday	75
Sunday	55

Complete the bar chart showing the number rented on Friday, Saturday and Sunday.

2

1 mark

Total marks for this topic

4

Line graphs

1 Lucy was ill in April. This is her temperature chart.

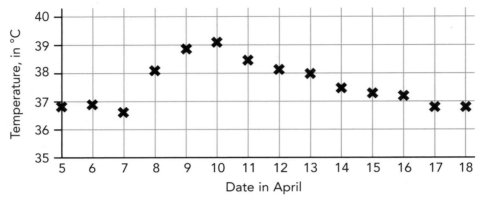

a) For how many days was Lucy's temperature more than 37°C?

b) Estimate Lucy's highest temperature shown on the graph.

Give your answer to one decimal place. [ ] °C

2 These two graphs show the rainfall reading and the temperature reading during one week.

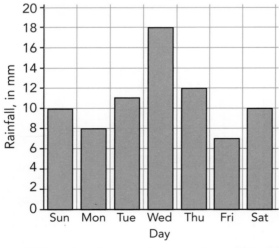 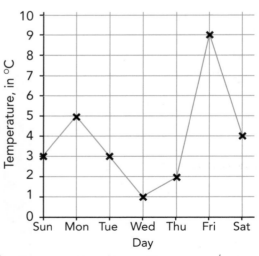

a) Use both graphs to describe what the weather was like on Wednesday.

b) Use both graphs to compare the weather on Wednesday and Friday.

3 Asif measured the length of a shadow every 30 minutes during the day and made a graph to show how the length changed.

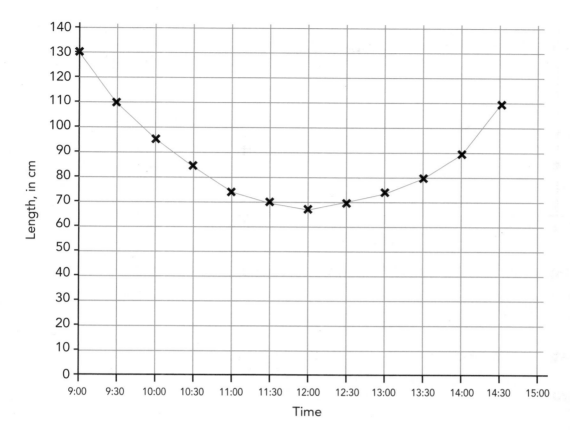

a) When was the shadow the longest?

3a

1 mark

b) When was the shadow the shortest?

3b

1 mark

c) Write down two times when the shadow length was the same.

3c

1 mark

d) What do you think the shadow length might be at 15:00?

3d

1 mark

Total marks for this topic

Thank you for buying this book!

Rising Stars publish a fantastic range of books and software. You can find out more on our website at www.risingstars-uk.com.

We'd love to hear what you think about this book. Email your comment to us at joannemitchell@risingstars-uk.com.